Becoming A Better You

Kimberly Moses

Copyright © 2019 by Kimberly Moses

All rights reserved. No part of this publication may be reproduced by any means, graphics, electronic, or mechanical, including photocopying, recording, taping, or by any information storage retrieval system without the written permission of the publisher except in the case of brief quotations embodied in critical articles and reviews.

Kimberly Moses/Rejoice Essential Publishing

PO BOX 512

Effingham, SC 29541

www.republishing.org

Unless otherwise indicated, scripture is taken from the King James Version.

Scripture quotations marked (ESV) are taken from The Holy Bible, English Standard Version® (ESV®) Copyright © 2001 by Crossway, a publishing ministry of Good News Publishers. All rights reserved.

Becoming A Better You/ Kimberly Moses

ISBN-13: 978-1-952312-08-3

Library of Congress Control Number: 2020935501

Dedication

This book wouldn't be possible without the inspiration of the Holy Spirit. This manuscript took five years to complete as the Lord allowed me to go through various trials and warfare.

2 Timothy 3:16-17 says, "All scripture is given by inspiration of God, and is profitable for doctrine, for reproof, for correction, for instruction in righteousness: That the man of God may be perfect, thoroughly furnished unto all good works."

Table of Contents

ACKNOWLEDGEMENTS...................ix

INTRODUCTION...............................1

CHAPTER 1:   Kingdom Focused............5

CHAPTER 2:   Take Steps To Grow Spiritually.............16

CHAPTER 3:   Write Down Goals...........23

CHAPTER 4:   Eat Better And Exercise...................38

CHAPTER 5:   Love On You...................47

CHAPTER 6:   Cut the Negativity..........55

CHAPTER 7:   Let it Go..........................63

ABOUT THE AUTHOR....................72

Acknowledgements

Thank you to my husband, Tron, for always pushing me to go further.

Thank you to Pastor Kevin Brewer for giving me a prophetic word to write this book.

Thank you to those who are a part of my virtual writing group. The hard work paid off and now you guys see the manifestation of our writing classes.

Introduction

Will anything good ever come out of this? Will my life ever get better? I don't see my way out of this situation. I have been praying, fasting, and believing God for a breakthrough, but nothing has happened. These were some of my thoughts as I was going through the darkest moments of my life. I was established and had financial security, but one bad decision led to others. I had lost my five-bedroom house and downgraded to a one-bedroom apartment. I lost my good paying job and barely worked. Everything that I ever knew was gone. There was no shoulder to cry on or no one to depend on. I was lost and hopeless. I was full of rage and I hated my ex-husband for mistreating me. I tried to get revenge, but that action landed me on two years of probation. I couldn't believe that I was stuck in an unfamiliar state to complete my probation and to go through a divorce. There were days that I felt lonely and depressed. My life was a mess and I was at rock bottom.

One day, I had a breaking point after I had got arrested and violated my probation. I knew that if I continued on that dark path, then I would be dead or in prison. So, I cried out to God and He showed me how to be a better person. I had to be delivered from fear because it was destroying my life and causing hindrances to fulfilling my destiny. I had to release unforgiveness, anger, and the pain I felt towards my ex-husband. After I did these things, then I was able to walk on the road to recovery and embrace the prophetic call on my life. During my fourth year of ministry, the Lord gave me a teaching series called, "Becoming a Better You." I would write a blog and then do a video on it afterward. Many people were blessed, and a pastor even gave me a prophetic word. He said, "I see this series becoming a book." At the time that I received that word, I brushed it off because I wanted the series to stay a blog and not become a book. Another year passed and more books were authored but I kept going back to that prophetic word. I had no other choice but to write it.

Every day, I witness people who are stagnant in their walk with the Lord. They have no spiritual growth and aren't progressing in their faith walk. It's sad to say that they are 'babes' in Christ even though they may have been saved for a while or a churchgoer for many years. They haven't been trained and lack the power of God from their lives. One of my biggest prayers is to be productive and effective. I enjoy empowering people to become better. The Lord gave me a list of seven steps to achieve success and if you follow them, you will produce the fruit of the Holy Spirit. These steps are:

1. Kingdom Focused
2. Take Steps To Grow Spiritually

3. Write down goals/make steps to achieve them
4. Eat Better And Exercise
5. Love On You
6. Cut the Negativity
7. Let it Go

Each chapter consists of thought-provoking questions to help you grow spiritually. As I reflect on how far the Lord has brought me, I know I am a better person. I am not full of anger anymore. When people try me or get an attitude with me, I don't get one back. When challenges arise, I don't worry because I know that the Lord will come through for me. When I go through warfare, my perspective is different than before. I used to see attacks as a bad thing, but now it means a major door is about to open or promotion (1 Corinthians 16:9). You don't have to stay bitter, but you can become better. My friend, get ready to experience life-changing revelation that will shift your mind and cause miraculous breakthroughs in your life.

CHAPTER ONE

Kingdom Focused

As we go along on this journey, sometimes we lose focus. We forget how passionate we used to be for the Lord. Remember when you first got saved. Did you read your Bible in public? Did you smile often while telling others about Jesus? Did you skip your lunch break to pray and read the Word? Were you excited about your journey with the Lord? My answer to all these questions is yes. However, along the way, I got distracted by the cares of this life and became carnal. I started watching reality shows and stopped focusing on the things of God. I was bitter and angry. I became one of those women that I had been watching on reality television. If your journey is similar, there is hope for you.

Have you gotten discouraged because of the trials and lost focus? I did before and I tried to take matters into my own hands only to fail miserably. When we lose focus because of our circumstances in life, we tend to forget the reason for our faith and the basics of Christianity. I told God that I was going back to the basics, which was to spread the name of Jesus Christ throughout the earth. Years have gone by and I kept my vow to the Lord. I could have many conferences such as a prophetic meeting or women's empowerment to draw a larger crowd, but I only want to do one.

"Empowering the New Me," is a conference that lifts up the name of Jesus. I remember doing my first prophetic conference at my local church. It was full because everyone wanted a Word from God. Then a couple of months later, I did a prayer conference at the same church and it was half full. I felt disheartened because other religions pray for hours. When I was a Buddhist in my youth, I chanted for hours. Why can't believers in Jesus come together to pray and communicate with our creator? I'm not looking for a crowd or affirmation of others. I don't want people to seek me out because I'm a prophet instead of seeking God. I decided to do the "Empowering the New Me" conference regardless of who comes because this faith walk is about focusing on Jesus. Focusing on Jesus is a part of being Kingdom-minded. I discovered that Jesus is my strength and source of peace as I focus on Him (Is. 26:3).

You don't have to be behind the pulpit to tell others about Jesus. Many people feel like they need a title or credentials to witness to the lost. We don't need a microphone to preach the gospel and to do work for the Lord. I observed some of the greatest encounters of the power of God manifesting outside of the four walls of the church. Even in being overwhelmed by my day's busy schedule, the Lord can speak a word of knowledge to me for someone I will cross paths with at the gas station, the post office, or the grocery store. I recall a time when I was at the post office shipping out packages of my books to some of my devoted supporters. I felt flustered because of my packed work schedule and I yearned to get home quickly. A sickly faint woman stood in the line ahead of me at the clerk's counter. It was apparent that she had been discharged from the hospital because she still had the patient wrist band on her feeble arm. She appeared gray and exhausted. She desperately needed help as she slowly searched for money in her pocketbook to pay for the postage. Compassion went through me and I acted swiftly by offering to pay.

After the transaction was made, she was too incoherent to notice. The postal clerk knew that I was a minister because of previous conversations, so she nodded her head in approval of what I was about to do. I said, "Ma'am. Let's step over to the side so we won't be in anyone's way." I grabbed her hand, leading her to the other side of the building. I took the papers out of her hand, so they wouldn't fall and scattered across the floor. Immediately, the Spirit of God came upon me and both of us felt His presence. I started to prophesy and pray for her healing. Tears streamed down her eyes and she lifted the hand that I wasn't holding to heaven. She praised God as strength came back into her body. Many onlookers passed us by wondering what was occurring. They witnessed God's miraculous healing power. A few weeks went by and I saw her again in another store. I barely recognized her because she looked so different. She looked refreshed and well put together.

We are called to do the work of an evangelist (2 Timothy 4:5). I made a vow to always place a sinner's prayer in my magazine, "Rejoice Essential." I can preach and prophesy all day, but I want to lift up the name of Jesus more. However, we must keep on striving while keeping our eyes on the cross. What are you doing to lift up the name of Jesus? Do the people around you know that you are saved or a believer in Jesus Christ? Are you witnessing to the lost?

When I did this teaching on periscope, souls got saved. The Glory of God manifested, and people got healed. Many people came and testified about how they needed this teaching. I want to grow spiritually. Don't you? I want the Lord to be pleased with my life. Do you? I don't want to be distracted on this journey. Many people are sitting on the sidelines because of the challenges they face. They gave in to the discouragement, or the trials while putting everything on the back burner. Rise up! It's time to shift your mind to become a better you.

The first step in becoming a better you is to be Kingdom focused. When you are Kingdom focused, you don't have time to be caught up in nonsense. There are many scandals in the body of Christ. The Holy Spirit is beyond grieved. You don't have time to worry about what God is doing in someone else's ministry when you are focused on your own assignment from Him. There is no need for jealousy or strife, which is one of the most appalling spirits because it will make you bitter and usher in competition with the people that you should be learning from. It will have you missing God and your next level. Some doors don't open until the Lord sends the right person to favor you. When you are kingdom-focused, you are focused solely on God's business. You only want what He wants and nothing more.

What is Kingdom focused? It is becoming knowledgeable of the Kingdom of God. The

Kingdom is synonymous with the Kingdom of heaven. When you know the identity of God, you will gain a deeper revelation of Him. It's a process that can occur over time as we spend time with the Lord. Are you willing to go through this process? The Kingdom is where we can draw the line between the children of God and the children of darkness.

Romans 8:9 says, "...Now if anyone does not have the Spirit of Christ, he is not His."

When we are Kingdom focused, we allow God to rule over our hearts and lives because we are submitted to His authority. We are taking the time and sacrifice to yield to our sovereign God. Did you know that the Kingdom of God is within you? Jesus revealed this in His answer to the Pharisee's question about the kingdom (Luke 17:21). Let's take the steps to make sure that everywhere we go, God goes. I want to take God with me in the grocery store, restaurant, school, work, etc. I decided to take the necessary steps to strengthen the kingdom within me.

Did you know that the Kingdom of God is strong? Not even the attacks of hell will be able to prevail against it! The prophet Daniel said in Daniel 2:44, "The God of heaven would set up a kingdom that will never be destroyed."

It's time to check ourselves. It's time to realize who we are in God. It's time to get some understanding. God's Kingdom is established, and He rules over all (Psalm 103:19; 45:6; 145:11-13). Just as the disciples of Jesus preached the Kingdom, so should we. Not only should we preach it, but we should also be able to demonstrate it. When we take a closer look at Matthew 10:7-8, we see some signs that the Kingdom of God has come. When it comes, the sick will get healed, the lepers will get cleanse, the dead will be raised, and demons will get cast out. When I started focusing on God's Kingdom, I began walking in greater authority. Signs and wonders just followed me. There was an ease and I just walked in it. I didn't have to try to force anything to happen. God honored my word and responded to my cries during prayer, worship, and preaching. When I try not to prophesy, the Lord fills my mouth with a new song from heaven or with His

Word. Now forget all the foolishness that may be going on around you. Let's get Kingdom focused and experience a move of God! Lives are waiting for us to demonstrate the Kingdom of God!

1. What is being Kingdom-minded?

   _____
   _____
   _____
   _____
   _____

2. Are your thoughts focused on God's Kingdom? If not, what steps will you take for your mind to focus on God's agenda on the earth?

   _____
   _____
   _____
   _____
   _____

3. What are the strongest gifts in your life? What are you talented at doing? How can you use these things to advance God's Kingdom?

_____
_____
_____
_____
_____

4. What are some supernatural things would you like to experience in your life, family, ministry, workplace or business?

_____
_____
_____
_____
_____

5. What are some areas you failed to demonstrate God's Kingdom and what lessons did you learn?

_____
_____
_____
_____
_____

CHAPTER TWO

Write Down Goals

Many people have ideas but don't know how to get started. They want to write books and plays. They desire to start businesses, organizations, and ministries. They feel like they don't have enough resources to get started, so time goes by and nothing gets accomplished.

Habakkuk 2:2 tells us to write the vision and make it plain. We have to be specific and tell the

Lord exactly what we want. The Holy Spirit will tell us exactly what to do as we seek Him. He gives us gifts as He leads us into all truth. Whenever the Lord gives me an idea, I write it down, so I don't lose it. I don't want to miss out on what the Lord has for me.

Vision is very important because without it we are blind and often scattered. Without vision, the people perish (Proverbs 29:18). We must ask the Lord for prophetic insight in order to stay on task. As the Lord gives me books, I visualize the outline. I can see the film playing in my mind as I write scripts. I receive visions on what steps I need to take to build various projects.

MAKE STEPS TO ACHIEVE THEM

Sometimes we get ahead of God and we don't even acknowledge Him when we make plans. Then when things go wrong, we finally pray. I made this mistake in business and in bad relationships. I learned the hard way to pray about everything and everyone.

Psalm 37:5 says, "Commit thy way unto the LORD; trust also in him; and he shall bring it to pass."

When God gives you a plan, yield it to Him, then trust Him to bring it to pass. When God gives you a vision, you need His help to accomplish it. The vision God gives us is big and goes over our heads, which is why we should depend on Him. When God gave me the idea for the publishing company, I had no idea where to begin. I prayed and fasted for directions. Then I did a lot of research and God provided the provisions for the startup cost. I dedicated my business to Him, and He always ensured that I had plenty of clientele.

Proverbs 16:3 (ESV) Commit your work to the LORD, and your plans will be established.

The Lord gave me six steps of vision building:

- Make Goals

People who have no goals in life just sit around wasting time. They live a life full of regrets. If not careful, they will end up envious of others who are succeeding while missing out on their own assignment.

- Plan It

This step includes researching startup costs, certifications, laws, and other requirements.

- Implement It

When we implement something, then we just do it and not just talk about it. Some people like to do a lot of talking but never make any moves. We invest, enroll, go forth, etc.

- Obtain It

You have to finish what you started. Once you begin make up your mind to see the end goal, you will get the certification, finished product, or achievement.

- Be Consistent

You can never give up during the difficulties. Anything great is worth hard work. The devil always resists God-given assignments.

- Network

We have to surround ourselves with people who are where we want to be so they can motivate us and bring the right connections in our life. Iron sharpens iron. We must learn from them.

1. How important is writing down your goals and having a vision for your life?

_____
_____
_____
_____
_____

2. Which of the six steps of vision building would you like to improve in and why?

_____
_____
_____
_____
_____

3. Where do you see yourself in the next five years? What is your plan to ensure your success?

_____
_____
_____
_____
_____

4. Evaluate the people in your life. List them into two categories: positive or negative. If they encourage you to succeed, place them into the positive category. If they discourage you, place them into the negative category.

5. Have you ever started something and didn't finish? If so, what will you do to ensure you complete the task now?

CHAPTER THREE

Take Steps To Grow Spiritually

Each year we should be growing in our faith. There should be an indication of the growth of the fruit that is produced in our lives. For instance, I was a pew warmer or someone who went to church and did nothing for ten years. That's a lot of time wasted. I didn't want to volunteer or serve. I had no clue about the gifts of the Spirit. I barely prayed or read the Bible. I was as cold as an ice pick. I wasn't growing spiritually, and my heart was hard towards the things of God. I failed to take steps to grow spiritually. Does this sound like you or someone else you might know? I realized that time is valuable, and we can't get it back, so let's make the most of it.

I always tell women, it doesn't do any good to have beauty without a brain; beautiful without anointing equals ineffective. This was my case for many years. I was caught up in looks and physical gain but was ignorant of the Word of God. I couldn't even heal a headache if I prayed. I didn't realize how superficial beauty truly was because, as we age, looks will fade. Wrinkles and gray hairs will come. Our skin will sag. Our posture may not be as upright. I discovered over time that true beauty comes from within. A woman can be beautiful on the outside, but if her heart is evil, she is an ugly person. As I grew in God, He placed an anointing upon my life, and it made me even more attractive. The anointing draws favor and causes people to like you. Sometimes, people don't even know why they are drawn to me. The anointing is like a bright light and attracts attacks from the enemy.

I can look back and see how much I have grown spiritually. I recall a time when I was embarrassed because I was asked to pray publicly by a married couple in a prayer meeting. I had no clue what to say. When I lost everything in 2014, I finally decided to get serious about my relationship with God. God started speaking to me and instructed me to do YouTube Videos. "No way, God! I have bad anxiety! I can't even speak in front of people without shaking." I wrestled with God and He won. I started my channel on YouTube and God has used that platform to draw people to the ministry. Many people have testified, "I never heard of you, but then you popped up on YouTube." These people had no idea how much of a struggle with my confidence in speaking on camera. Yet I stayed faithful, and God's presence overwhelms me each time I minister on a video.

These are the mandatory steps that I took to grow spiritually: Praying, fasting, worshipping, studying the word, and living holy. It's amazing how much we can grow when we are thrown right into the midst of the fire. This is why some parents throw their babies into the pool so they can learn how to swim. It's shocking to see, but it works. The baby immediately starts kicking and begins to float. Well, this is how I learned to pray, during the storm. I was being attacked financially, relationally, legally, mentally, and the list goes on. I learned how to pray fervently. Prayer became a part of my DNA. Sometimes, the Lord gives me a burden for prayer. I have to pray until I get a release or until the peace comes back again. Often, I can feel when I'm under attack or when someone is praying against me. I rebuke it immediately and pray intensely in the tongues because the Holy Spirit makes intercession for us.

After I went through a python attack, I decided to step up my prayer life, so I launched, "Tongues of Fire," at 6 am where we pray in tongues for one-hour Monday through Fridays. Then to give the devil an extra punch, I launched a prayer movement where we pray again at noon. As I pray often, it's not a struggle to prophesy or enter the presence of the Lord. Many testimonials have come forth from the prayer line. We have seen many healings and deliverances. God shows up and out. Imagine how much fruit you will have when you step up your prayer life?

The next step to grow spiritually is fasting. Fasting has worked wonders in my walk. It has totally killed my fleshly lusts and desires. There were so many situations where I could've sin, but my love for God was so strong. God can keep the singles if they want to be kept. When I was single, I fasted a lot and stayed before the Lord so I wouldn't fall into temptation. My relationship with God is the top priority. Even when the devil presented temptation before me, I rebuked it, and my flesh didn't budge. This is how Jesus was in the wilderness (Luke 4). He was on a forty-day fast. The tempter came to tempt him with various things to which many people would've succumb. Yet, Jesus combatted the temptation with the Word of God and gained strength from fasting. I incorporated fasting into my lifestyle and it has shifted me.

Matthew 6:16 tells us not to be like hypocrites when we fast by looking sad or indicating you're fasting. No one knows that I am fasting except my spouse, so we can be on one accord or my mentees because we corporately fast together. We have to learn how to build in secret and let others watch the results. If we tell the wrong person we are fasting, they might try to shake our faith. Fasting is scriptural. Ester fasted and received favor with the King. King Jehoshaphat fasted and got the victory. Daniel fasted and had a breakthrough. The disciples fasted and worked miracles. I have many documented miracles, and some can be witnessed by watching the replay of my periscope, YouTube, or Facebook videos. I have seen limbs grow out evenly, deaf ears open, lumps dissolving, demons leave, salvations, and limbs straighten. Fasting produces power.

In Matthew 17:21, Jesus reveals that some spirits only come out by prayer and fasting. Don't you want to be powerful in God? I desire to know the God of Elijah, Smith Wigglesworth, and other saints. Whenever we study Isaiah 58, we can see the benefits of fasting. Don't be a powerless Christian! If witches, warlocks, and people of other religions fast, why can't God's children? I refuse to let a witch outdo me in the spirit. If they are fasting for one hour a day, I will do the whole day.

The next step to grow spiritually is worshipping the Lord. I love to worship and can do so for many hours. I, even, have my husband loving some of my classic worship songs, which usher in the presence of God every time. The Lord has given me my own music and, at first, I was so afraid to sing them. After spending lots of time in the wilderness, I didn't care if people didn't like my singing. They didn't suffer or die on the cross for me. I have to sing unto God to get my breakthrough. I can't get enough of His presence. I don't want to have a trickle of His presence. I want to carry His presence everywhere because it makes a difference. I can tell the level of authority a person walks in by the amount of presence coming off their lives. Every time I worship, I feel God's fire and I receive revelation. My mind spins with so many ideas and creativity. I always tell the Lord that I can't wait to build what He shows me in the spirit.

When the people of Antioch worshipped in Acts 13, they received their next move. They knew that Paul and Barnabus had to separate. If you want clarity or direction, go into worship. Our worship goes beyond listening to music but into our lifestyles. We see this in Romans 12. Live a life that is pleasing to God; it is your reasonable service. Worship brings in the harvest. The Holy Spirit told me these words many years ago and they have been proven true. I have many testimonies of being broke, but after I worshipped, the money was there. Once, I needed to go to a birthday party but didn't have any gas money, so I sang to the Lord then I heard a notification go off on my phone. It was an email from PayPal telling me that someone sowed a seed. The riches are in the Glory, so learn how to get a hold of God and you will never be broke.

The next step to grow spiritually is studying the Word. There are so many resources available. There are study Bibles, devotionals, websites, classes, and trainings to help you study God's Word effectively. There is no excuse for not studying the Word especially when information is readily available via the internet. We are told to study unto God in 2 Timothy 2:15. 2 Peter 1:10 tells us to try hard to make your calling and election sure. If you are truly chosen by God to do a great work, then there should be a desire to want to study and learn. When the Holy Spirit told me that I was going to have a healing and deliverance ministry, I read many books about it. When He told me that I was a prophet, I went and started an extensive study on biblical prophets. I want to excel at what I'm called to do, don't you? Studying is for your benefit. The Word of God provides teaching, instructions for righteousness, correction, and reproof (2 Tim. 3:16-17).

I remember I asked God, "Lord, give me a word for your people." The Lord replied, "You don't have a word because you haven't been in my Word." When I heard the Lord tell me this, I was so convicted. God wasn't speaking to me because I wasn't taking time to study His thoughts and His heart in the Bible. Many prophets are prophesying from the flesh and scratching itching ears. God doesn't want that for us. He wants us to speak what is truly on His heart and mind for an individual. I obeyed the Lord and committed to reading at least one chapter every day before I go to bed and it has increased the prophetic anointing upon my life. There were times when I got in the Word and the Lord began to reveal the secrets of men or those connected to me. Once, He said, "___ sinned last night. Go ask her." So, I stopped reading the Word and I reached out to the young lady. "The Lord told me you sinned last night." She confessed and that was an opportunity for me to minister to her about not falling into sexual sins. If you want to hear the voice of God more in your life, then get in the Word.

The last step in growing spiritually is living holy. Holiness attracts God's presence. He wants to dwell in a pure place. Don't grieve the Holy Spirit with sin. The Holy Spirit is grieved in our lives by the people who surround us, the things we listen to, or the things we watch on television. As I grow in God, my spirit becomes more sensitive where things bother me that might not affect others in the same way. For instance, if I watch a movie with the spirit of violence in it, then later that night, that spirit may try to come to attach itself to me. I can hear and feel it. Then I have to pray until it leaves me alone. It's almost like God has my spirit on high alert so I can see the enemy that's hiding. I decided a long time ago that it's not worth vexing the Holy Spirit. I walk in peace so when the peace starts to lift then I know something is wrong.

Holiness is not based on appearances such as long priestly garments, robes, dresses, or not wearing makeup. I have seen women who were perceived as the church whores in the congregation because some of the brothers boasted that they 'hit that' or 'ran through that.' These women wore the long skirts that I wasn't willing to wear. So, your outer appearance does not guarantee your dedication to solidarity with God. When I got saved at the age of twenty-one, I attended a Pentecostal church or 'holiness denomination,' where women weren't allowed to wear pants and cut their hair. I didn't do too well in this setting.

Holiness is determined if the door to sin is closed in someone's life. I got a revelation of righteousness when I had an encounter with God one day. I was worshipping and His glory pinned me down to the floor. My eyes began to open in the spirit and His hand came down out of the ceiling. He handed me a scepter of righteousness. "Take this scepter of righteousness and teach my people about it." When the Lord spoke those words to me, I received the fear of the Lord in my heart. I didn't want to sin against Him anymore. I decided not to compromise, and I wrote the book, "In Right Standing: A Daily Devotional." I dissociated from the carnal preachers who were cursing and fornicating. I knew that I couldn't play around with God anymore. God was calling me into prophetic ministry, I got on fire and slammed the door hard in the devil's face. I started living what I was preaching. I wanted to be the real deal meaning a true prophet of God. I claimed my house for Jesus and His presence dwells there. Whenever I minister, He comes like rushing wind and ready to pour out His spirit. Leviticus 20:7 tells us to consecrate ourselves and live holy. It is a commandment to live holy (1 Peter 1:16). It's time to say goodbye to sin and people that are hindering your spiritual growth.

Make a decision to apply these steps in your life. We all have room for improvement. When you think you have mastered something in God, you will quickly discover that there is another level. Some people are really strong in one area but struggle in another area. I applied all these steps and within three years, God accelerated me in the spirit. Remember, spiritual maturity isn't based on age. You can be 65 but be immature in the natural. You can be 19 and be spiritually mature. In review, prayer, fasting, worshipping, studying the word, and living holy involves taking steps to grow spiritually. Let's take some steps!

1. Do you feel stagnant in your spiritual walk? If so, what steps will you take for growth?

_____

_____

_____

_____

_____

2. Compare your spiritual walk with the previous year. What areas have you failed or seen minimum growth? Write down a plan to help you succeed.

_____

_____

_____

_____

_____

3. Which mandatory steps (prayer, fasting, worshipping, studying the word, and living holy) that were discussed are a part of your life? Which ones do you need to invest more effort in and how can you apply them to your life?

_____

_____

_____

_____

_____

4. What impact are you making on the lives around you? Are you influencing them in a godly or ungodly way? What would they say about you if someone were to ask them about you?

_____

_____

_____

5. Read Galatians 5:22-23. Which fruits of the Spirit are you lacking in your life? How can you increase in these areas?

CHAPTER FOUR
Eat Better And Exercise

It may be tough during the holiday season or celebrations to eat healthy and exercise but it's possible. I learned to eat in moderation so I can enjoy the foods that I love. Afterward, I stick to my exercise routine. Whenever we eat healthier and exercise, we feel better about ourselves. Our self-esteem increases as we look better in our clothes. Exercising helps us stay toned and healthy. Imagine how good you will look and feel after working out for a length of time?

I gained fifty pounds when I got remarried because I rarely exercised and cooked more. I felt horrible. My husband loves the curves, but I knew that I wasn't happy. I used to work out at least three times per week when I lived in Colorado. I had maintained 125 lbs. for years. Then I got up to 168 lbs., which was the same weight that I was when I gave birth to my two children. How can I be the exact weight and I'm not even pregnant? There were times that I felt bloated. People mistook me for carrying a child, asking: "When are you due?" I would smile and say, "Oh, no. I'm not pregnant." They would then apologize. At first, it hurt my feelings, but then I used it as a motivating factor. I refused to buy bigger jeans, tops, and other garments. I put my foot down and took steps to change. I started drinking more water and that was a struggle. It used to take a whole day to drink one 16.8 oz. bottle of water now I can drink two or three. My goal is to drink a gallon of water a day, so I can eat less.

At first, I didn't know how to balance everything with marriage, motherhood, and having a business. My schedule during the day is busy, so exercising at night is better. I made up many excuses to not workout, but I've learned to just do it.

When we eat better and exercise, we digest food more efficiently. I used to get indigestion often until the Lord healed me. I always felt so sick after I ate a meal. Now, it has been many years and those problems are far behind me. Eating certain foods weighs us down, causes constipation and diseases such as hypertension, diabetes, or myocardial infarction. I decided to cut back my meat intake because it causes sluggishness sometimes.

I can recall how I felt during my postpartum period. I felt miserable because my stomach was still the shape of a flattened cone from where the baby was located. I had to work really hard to get back to my pre-pregnancy weight. People used to always compliment me on my slimness. They were so surprised that I have children.

The Lord dealt with me pertaining this subject matter years ago. So many of God's children are a knife and fork away from the grave. They are a hamburger away from a heart attack. They have a hard time preaching the Word without getting winded because of the extra weight. I have seen preachers sitting down in a chair for the entirety of the sermon because they can't bear their body weight on their legs. If they do stand then their ankles will swell. I also saw another minister who had to be hooked up to an oxygen tank to preach because of t shortness of breath when overly exerted. I decided to be in physical shape, so I can preach the gospel without my health causing a hindrance. When I minister, I will wear my heels and no matter how bad my feet hurt, I will work those heels unto the Lord. Many of God's servants die prematurely due to health issues such as obesity, heart attacks, strokes, diabetes, and so on.

It always bothered me when a minister would have a meeting and everyone in attendance didn't receive prayer or prophecy. I told God that I want to make sure that everyone at my meetings receives ministry. This is the reason I am passionate about health. I am ready to flow with the Holy Spirit whenever He wants to flow. Once I get in the flow, I will be ready to lay hands on a few hundred people if the Lord wants. We have to be ready in season and out of season. We have to be in better health to do the work of the Lord.

This is the reason I always feature a healthy recipe inside Rejoice Essential Magazine monthly. You can find various recipes in the Healthy Living section. I featured vegetarian lasagna, salads, seafood, poultry, and the list goes on and on. I even introduced my husband to some vegetarian recipes that he enjoyed. He finds himself hungry again after a couple of hours because the dishes are lighter than what he is used to; however, over time the body adjusts, and the recipes are fulfilling. Vegetables are lower in calories and we can eat a lot of them without feeling guilty.

God wants us to prosper in every way and be healthy in the process. 3 John 2 says, "Beloved, I wish above all things that thou mayest prosper and be in health, even as thy soul prospereth. We have to realize that it's about God and not us. Our bodies are His temple. God wants to dwell in a healthy body. 1 Corinthians 3:16 says, "Know ye not that ye are the temple of God, and that the Spirit of God dwelleth in you?" Remember, it's not about you but God's glory. We are not our own. We have been bought with a price.

1 Corinthians 6:19-20 says, "What? know ye not that your body is the temple of the Holy Ghost which is in you, which ye have of God, and ye are not your own? For ye are bought with a price: therefore glorify God in your body, and in your spirit, which are God's." There are many recalls of foods and some of the chemicals in it are killing us. Say goodbye to processed foods and prepare your own delicious meals. Forget the sodas and drink more water. Find alternate healthier recipes for your favorite foods. Make a commitment to become a better you. Let's eat better and exercise. Let's live longer and do what God is calling us to do.

1. Are you taking care of your body? Explain the ways you are or not.

   _____
   _____
   _____
   _____
   _____

2. Make a list of food items and drinks you consume daily. Place them into two categories: more or less. If something isn't healthy place it into the less category. If something is nutritious then place it into the more category. Visit Choosemyplate.gov to get the recommended serving amounts.

   _____
   _____
   _____
   _____
   _____

3. Get your favorite processed food out of your pantry or research them online. Look up the ingredients. Do you know the chemicals used that make them up and their effects on your health? Can you pronounce the ingredients? Are any of the ingredients used in other products that aren't edible such as cleaning agents or pesticides?

_____
_____
_____
_____
_____

4. Are you feeling insecure about your body? If so, how can you get over the insecurities?

_____
_____
_____
_____
_____

5. Are you physically fit to preach the gospel and to travel? If not, develop a diet and workout plan to accommodate your schedule.

_____
_____
_____
_____
_____

CHAPTER FIVE

Love On You

Loving you is an important aspect in life. When you love yourself, you have standards! People will no longer be allowed to mistreat you or walk all over you. You will no longer allow people to abuse you. When I learned to say no to people and put boundaries in place, it felt so good. I wasn't overwhelmed or burdened. I wasn't distracted and I could focus on my God-given assignments. I was able to spend time with God and regroup so I could be more effective in what I'm called to do. People will drain you and then kick you to the curve. Part of self-care is making sure that you are balanced emotionally, spiritually, and physically.

Loving you involves treating yourself. Well, when was the last time that you did something nice for yourself? I am committed to getting my hair done every couple of months so I can feel beautiful. I make sure I get an outfit for special occasions so I can always look my best. Sometimes, I run a nice hot bubble bath to soak and give myself a pedicure. My husband and I order our favorite takeout and cuddle, so our emotional needs are met. I, even, play games on my phone to take breaks so I won't burn out during a long workday.

Three years ago, I declared over myself that I would start loving me. Before then, I was severely depressed and just going about the normal routine such as work, dropping the kids to school, and church. My life was inundated with menial tasks. The only focus was "doing" but I had no social life, no fun, no new wardrobe and the list continues. I totally let myself go. Prayer was given for everyone except myself. When was the last time you prayed for yourself? Many moms and wives totally neglect themselves after marriage and parenthood. I was one of them.

Don't neglect yourself. After making those declarations, I began to love myself. I didn't have a lot of money at the time, so I did a lot of things at home. I did my own facials and deep conditioning treatments. I cooked my favorite meals. Prior to that, I made up excuses not to cook, such as me being single. I went into the kitchen and cooked like I had a husband. I invested in myself. I brought a few new outfits because I was way overdue. I started exercising and made healthier choices.

I decided to forgive the people who hurt me. Forgiveness is necessary in order to truly love yourself. I refused to allow those old wounds and painful baggage to be connected to me any further. Learning to forgive was more important for me and not necessarily for the other person. Those who I was hurt by moved forward in life. I was the one stuck in the pain. Forgiveness is a process. The sign that I truly forgave them was that I could look at their picture and not feel any ill will rise up within me.

Ephesians 4:32 says, "And be ye kind one to another, tenderhearted, forgiving one another, even as God for Christ's sake hath forgiven you." When I decided to let it go, God healed me. I started to love my neighbor as myself. I actually feel sorry for some of these people because they, too, need the mercy of God when they get judged for their evil actions. Keep your heart pure and your hands clean. Some people struggle with loving others because they don't love themselves, which was my problem. But that changed when I allowed God to do a great work within me. Some people get so disappointed by others because they have unrealistic expectations. You can't expect a broken person to fully love you as a whole person would.

Romans 13:9 says, "For this, Thou shalt not commit adultery, Thou shalt not kill, Thou shalt not steal, Thou shalt not bear false witness, Thou shalt not covet; and if there be any other commandment, it is briefly comprehended in this saying, namely, Thou shalt love thy neighbour as thyself." Whenever you love on you, there is no time for foolish things. There is no room for adultery, murder, theft, lying, and coveting because there is a mandate to fulfill. When I embraced loving myself, I let go of my past mistakes. Many people are still bound by past mistakes and this isn't the will of God. We shouldn't entertain foolish conversations and not everything deserves a response. I learned a long time ago not to put myself on the same level with a demon because the devil is underneath my feet. Foolish debates aren't fruitful.

There is no condemnation in Christ when you are walking in the spirit (Romans 8:1). When I meditated on this Scripture, I was set free. When people came to me to gossip, I shut it down. I declared that I was no one's trash can. I didn't allow people to weigh me down with their garbage. I didn't want to feel bad anymore by allowing people to drain me spiritually with their problems that were out of my control. Don't allow people to weigh you down with their drama. People will constantly dump bad news on you if you let them. We have to be careful about this because when they finish, we are heavy and have to go into prayer to get peace again. When I started to love on me, I was drama free. Think of yourself as a jewel. You are valuable. It's time to love on you!

Now, repeat after me. "I decree and declare that I will love on me this year. I will forgive people that hurt me and move on with my life. I will invest in myself physically, emotionally, mentally, and spiritually. I will pray for myself. I will not neglect myself. I will laugh, treat myself, and enjoy life. I decree that God will bless me with my heart's desires this year."

1. How important is self-care and do you do it?

_____

_____

_____

_____

_____

2. What does your self-care regimen look like? If you don't have one how would you like it to look?

_____
_____
_____
_____
_____

3. When was the last time you had fun, laughed, and rested without thinking about work or responsibilities?

_____
_____
_____
_____
_____

4. Write down some ways you can respectfully tell people not to use you as a spiritual dumpster anymore. In other words, what will you tell the person who always makes you feel heavy and drains you? What will you tell the gossiper? What will you tell

the person who crosses healthy boundaries? What will you say to the person whose heart and motives aren't right?

_____

_____

_____

_____

_____

5. What areas in your life do you procrastinate? What can you do to move forward?

_____

_____

_____

_____

_____

CHAPTER SIX

Cut The Negativity

Cutting the negative junk out of our lives is necessary. Misery loves company but you have to put your foot down and say, "I will no longer associate myself with misery."

Baggage weighs us down. God wants us to be free. There's no better feeling than to have the peace of God. His presence feels so good to me. If we don't cut the negative things out of our lives, then we won't experience the fullness of God's peace and provision. When I chose to cut negative people out of my life, then my faith was no longer shaken.

Some people want to get me on the phone to talk and there's nothing wrong with that, but I can't. My schedule won't allow it because I have many jobs. I'm a publisher, author, wife, mother, minister, mentor, spiritual mother, magazine editor, and beauty consultant. Sometimes, I feel like I'm pulled in ten different directions. I have to be wise with my time to complete the tasks before me. I rather pray for someone, give them a prophetic word if God speaks to me for them and keep it moving.

Some people have gotten offended at me because they wanted to be my best friend, but when they realized that wasn't going to happen, then they came against me. I knew they were sent from the enemy to cause a distraction in the first place; that's the reason the Lord didn't allow them to get close to me. The right connections will bless you and add something of value to get you to the next level. However, the wrong connections will demote you and be a hindrance. How many people in your life are causing you to be stagnant?

When the wrong people are in your life, they will kill your faith. Not realizing that the devil is using them will get you out of alignment with God. I got tired of people giving me carnal advice when God told me the opposite. I knew that I couldn't heed to the negative voices and still believe the promises of the Lord. Worldly people will tell you that you are crazy for trusting God. God called me off my job in 2016 to do ministry full time. I was no longer employed by man but by God. When I went through financial challenges, people would say, "Why don't you just get a job." I would reply, "God didn't tell me to get one, so I will trust Him." They wouldn't understand spiritual matters because of their carnal minds.

I had to cut the negativity. God can give me what I need. I truly depend on Him. God blessed me with more money in a day than what I made in one month. I learned to never doubt Him. 1 Corinthians 15:33 says, "Be not deceived: evil communications corrupt good manners." I know that I am going somewhere in God, so I can't have everyone in my ear. This should also be your mindset.

We can't carry any negativity where God is taking us. Say goodbye to carnality. It's hard to remain optimistic when you are surrounded by pessimistic people. 1 Corinthians 5:11 says, "But now I have written unto you not to keep company, if any man that is called a brother be a fornicator, or covetous, or an idolator, or a railer, or a drunkard, or an extortioner; with such an one no not to eat." We have to always be careful not to associate with people who blatantly try to cause us to sin against God. We can love those people from a distance, keep them in prayer, but we don't have to be best friends with them. Additionally, we have to guard the anointing on our lives because it was brought with a price.

Some doors won't open in your life until you disconnect from the wrong people. I remember I was connected to a false apostle who was cheating on his wife. He would snap and curse you out in a heartbeat. He had all the fruits of the devil but disguised himself as an angel of light. The Holy Spirit warned me so many times to block and delete him, but I didn't because I wanted to see the good in this person. I thought that if I ministered to him and prayed for him then he would change but I was wrong. He was deep in sin and the Lord didn't want me to be associated with that. So, I obeyed God and the next day, two doors opened for me. One was a television network and the other was international radio. I did both for a full year.

If we aren't careful, then we can get influenced by those we hang around. Have you ever had a friend mimic or copy you? Perhaps you admired a friend so much that you started acting and dressing like them over time. Well, we pick up attributes from those with whom we are associated. Years ago, I used to fellowship with a prophet. We chatted on the phone daily. This prophet had an attitude problem and didn't demonstrate the love of God. I noticed that one day, I was talking and acting like this person because of the time we spent together. Immediately I got convicted and prayed that I would love God's people and not mistreat them. That friendship with the prophet didn't work out because of their bitterness and ultimately, they fell into divination. I prayed for them until the Lord released me from that prayer assignment.

How many innocent pure vessels have you seen become tainted because they were influenced by people who didn't really love God? I have seen people start off right but over time, they became greedy just like the person they choose as mentors. We have to examine a person's fruit. If they aren't getting you closer to God, then it's time to re-evaluate their purpose in your life. Cutting away all negative sources from your life, will enable you to accomplish many things and obtain all that God has for you.

1. How do you feel when there is a bunch of drama around you? Do you feed off it and entertain it? Or do you feel vexed and annoyed by it?

_____

_____

_____

_____
_____

2. How important are connections in your life? Is there anything or anyone blocking the right connections in your life?

_____
_____
_____
_____
_____

3. Is there anyone that you need to forgive? If so, write down a prayer with their name and offense then pray aloud.

_____
_____
_____
_____
_____

4. Are there any sources (environment/people) of negativity in your life? What will you do to cut it away from you?

_____
_____
_____
_____
_____

5. Read Matthew 7:15-20. Examine the fruit of others in your life. Who can you trust? Who supports your vision? Who stood with you during the trials? Who can be honest with you even if it hurts? Who prays and encourages you?

_____
_____
_____
_____
_____

CHAPTER SEVEN

Let It Go

Do you want to operate in the supernatural? Well, the key is to let certain things go, such as fear. One day I was on Periscope recording, "The Making of A Prophet" series and God dissolved a lump that was the size of an egg in a woman's breast. At first, it didn't seem like anything was happening because of the resistance of the enemy. However, the more everyone prayed on the broadcast, the lump got smaller and smaller. Eventually, the lump disappeared in less than a two-hour time frame. That's God! I couldn't operate in miracles until I let go of some things. I had to let go of the fear of speaking in tongues and singing in public. My tongues didn't sound like everyone else's, so insecurity set in. I didn't realize that was the enemy trying to stop the Holy Spirit from making intercession for me. Speaking in tongues is like a muscle. The more you do it then, the stronger your tongues become and overtime, they will change as you are able to make different syllables, utterances, and pronunciations.

I stopped caring about singing on key when I realized that the songs God gave me were anointed and would set the captive free as they are sung. I held back for years when I was invited to preach somewhere. When the song would be on the tip of my lips, I shut it down and quenched the Holy Spirit. I had to go through many more trials to fully surrender and let go so God could have His way. Over the years, people have testified that they needed to hear the song of the Lord coming from me.

I also had to let go of the fear of not being liked by people. The desire to have favor with some of the popular preachers preoccupied me but when I met some of these people, I was disappointed. Some were rude, carnal, prideful, and self-centered. Others rejected me so I used these things as motivation to go harder for God. No matter how hard I tried to fit in, it never worked. I can't conform to be like someone else because I'd lose who God created me to be. I'm goofy, bubbly, hard, and ambitious in one package. Anything else isn't authentic to my personality. It's all about dying to self and allowing the Lord to do a greater work within me.

Once I let go of all my fears and insecurities, I experienced a greater realm of God's Glory! It's truly a process and didn't happen overnight but, with God, it's possible. Part of becoming a better you is letting go of old baggage because bringing it into your new season will cause a huge hindrance. This baggage can include unforgiveness, pain, offense, revenge, soul ties, and the list continues. Ephesians 4:31 says, "Let all bitterness, and wrath, and anger, and clamour, and evil speaking, be put away from you, with all malice:" We can't enter into our new season carrying junk.

How are we able to receive the fullness of God if we are weighed down by these things? I want everything that God has for me. When someone hurts me, I don't always wait for an apology that may never come. I forgive them. I bless them. I love them from a distance. I won't look back and allow the enemy to place thoughts of regret in my mind. I have been hurt many times by the people that I helped the most. When they needed money, I gave. They called me for prayer when I was obligated to my family. They used me and cut me off. Many leaders don't want to train, mentor, and impart into others because of hurt. I learned that there are some good people who aren't out to get you but are assigned to you. We just have to guard our hearts, ask for discernment, and pray for the Lord to connect us with the right people. I will look forward and press towards the mark for the prize of the high calling of God in Christ Jesus (Philippians 3:14).

When you decide to let go and move forward, expect God to do a new thing in your life. Isaiah 43:18-19 says, "Remember ye not the former things, neither consider the things of old. Behold, I will do a new thing; now it shall spring forth;

shall ye not know it? I will even make a way in the wilderness, and rivers in the desert."

God makes it very clear not dwell on the past. He will supernaturally erase every traumatic event that has ever occurred. This is what happened to me. I had a conversation with my younger sister a couple of months ago. She was telling me about all the bad things that happened to us as children. In my shock, I couldn't remember any of it. It was as if God erased my memory of those painful childhood moments. I had truly let it go. God did such a new thing in my life that my past couldn't define me today. When God does a work, it's complete and perfect. There is no residue. People are shocked when they find that I was an exotic dancer, Buddhist, and had anger issues. Christ has truly delivered and transformed me into His image. We have to ask the Lord to take us through the sanctification process. Please don't skip this process.

When you let it go, be careful not to pick it back up again. Many people pray about a situation then worry about it later. They put their request on the altar then snatch it back by taking matters into their own hands and not waiting on God. God rebuked me once about this very issue. He asked, "Why come to me and pray if you will worry about it later?" I was so convicted but He was right. When I'm anxious about something, then most likely, I'm not ready for it. Yet when I rest in God, I forget that I prayed about it, and He blesses me with the very thing my prayers were centered on.

1 Peter 5:7 says, "Casting all your care upon him; for he careth for you." God loves us so much and He doesn't want us to worry about things that are out of our control. I constantly give all my concerns to God. It's amazing to see Him work out the issues in my life, all because I let it go and trusted Him. One of the hardest lessons that I learned in life is that I can't change anyone. I'm not God. All I can do is pray for them and believe that God will set them free. Many people are burned out because they have the Savior complex. We have to be careful that we don't make ourselves gods in people's lives. Don't let anyone worship you. Point them back to Jesus. God is a jealous God.

We have to be still and know that He is God. We have to realize how powerful He really is. When I let it go, I was no longer anxious about things that I couldn't control. Let every negative thing go and watch the amazing plans God has for you unfold. Jeremiah 29:11 says, "For I know the thoughts that I think toward you, saith the Lord, thoughts of peace, and not of evil, to give you an expected end." God has great things in store for you. Are you ready to let go of the things that are weighing you down so you can receive it?

1. What should you do when you are angry and want to confront someone? Explain your reasoning?

_____
_____
_____
_____
_____

2. Is God pleased when we take matters into our own hands? What does the Bible say about vindication? Do you believe God will fight for you?

_____
_____
_____
_____
_____

3. Do you struggle with double mindedness, doubt, and unbelief? What are some Scriptures that you can say to counteract these thoughts?

_____
_____
_____
_____
_____

4. What are some of the consequences of sin and making foolish decisions?

_____

_____

_____

_____

_____

5. Is there anything that you need you to let go of so you can experience the fullness of God in your life?

_____

_____

_____

_____

_____

About The Author

Kimberly Moses started off her ministry as Kimberly Hargraves. She is highly sought after as a prophetic voice, intercessor and prolific author. There is no doubt that she has a global mandate on her life to serve the nations of the world by spreading the Gospel of Jesus Christ. She has a quickly expanding worldwide healing and deliverance ministry. Kimberly Moses wears many hats to fulfill the call God has placed on her life as an entrepreneur over several businesses including her own personal brand Rejoice Essentials which promotes the Gospel of Jesus Christ.

She also serves as a life coach and mentor to many women. She is also the loving mother of two wonderful children. She is married to Tron. Kimberly has dedicated her life to the work of ministry and to serve others under the call God has placed over her life. Kimberly currently resides in South Carolina.

She is a very anointed woman of God who signs, miracles and wonders follow. The miraculous and incessant testimonies attributed to her ministry are incalculable, with many reporting physical and mental healing, financial breakthroughs, debt cancellations and other favorable outcomes. She is known across the globe as a servant who truly labors on behalf of God's people through intercession.

She is the author of The Following:

"Overcoming Difficult Life Experiences with Scriptures and Prayers"
"Overcoming Emotions with Prayers"
"Daily Prayers That Bring Changes"
"In Right Standing,"
"Obedience Is Key,"

"Prayers That Break The Yoke Of The Enemy: A Book Of Declarations,"
"Prayers That Demolish Demonic Strongholds: A Book Of Declarations,"
"Work Smarter. Not Harder. A Book Of Declarations For The Workforce,"
"Set The Captives Free: A Book Of Deliverance."
"Pray More Challenge"
"Walk By Faith: A Daily Devotional"
"Empowering The New Me: Fifty Tips To Becoming A Godly Woman"
"School of the Prophets: A Curriculum For Success"
"8 Keys To Accessing The Supernatural"
"Conquering The Mind: A Daily Devotional"
"Enhancing The Prophetic In You"
"The ABCs of The Prophetic: Prophetic Characteristics"
"Wisdom Is The Principal Thing: A Daily Devotional"
"It Cost Me Everything"
"The Making Of A Prophet: Women Walking in Prophetic Destiny"
"The Art of Meditation: A Daily Devotional"
"Warfare Strategies: Biblical Weapons"

You can find more about Kimberly at
www.kimberlyhargraves.com

For Rejoice Essential Magazine
www.rejoiceessential.com

For Beauty Products
www.rejoicingbeauty.com

Please write a review for my books on Amazon.com

Support this ministry:
Cashapp: $ProphetessKim
Paypal.me/remag

Index

A

anger, 2, 4, 65
anointing, 24–25, 58

B

babies, 26, 40
baggage, 55, 65
Barnabus, 30
bitter, 6, 10
bless, 52, 56, 66
Buddhist, 7, 67

C

certifications, 19
chemicals, 43, 45
Colorado, 39
Compassion, 8
conference, 7
congregation, 33
constipation, 40
conversations, 8, 67

D

Daniel, 28
darkest moments, 1
dark path, 2
deaf ears, 28
debt cancellations, 73
dedication, 33
delicious meals, 43
deliverances, 27, 74
demons, 12, 28, 51
devil, 27, 51, 57
diabetes, 40–41
discernment, 66
drama, 51, 60

E

enemy, 25, 64, 66, 74
entrepreneur, 72
evil actions, 50
exotic dancer, 67

F

faith, 6–7, 23, 28, 56–57, 74
fasting, 1, 27–29, 35
foolishness, 13
forgive, 49, 61, 66
fruit, 23, 27

G

garments, 33, 39
gospel, 41, 46, 72
grocery, 7, 11
growth, 35

H

healings, 27, 31

health, 41–42, 45
heart attacks, 41
hearts, 11, 24, 34, 50, 66

J

Jesus, 5–7, 9, 11–12, 27, 68

K

kingdom, 3, 5, 10–14

L

life, 1–2, 4–6, 14, 18, 20–21, 32, 34, 36–37, 47–49, 52, 54, 56–57, 60–62, 66–68, 71–73
love, 4, 27, 29, 38, 47, 49–52, 58

M

marriage, 40, 49
mentors, 56, 60
minister, 8, 25, 32, 41, 56
miracles, 64
misery, 55
money, 8, 30, 49, 57, 66

Moses, 2, 4, 6, 10, 12, 14, 18, 20, 22, 24, 26, 28, 30, 32, 72
music, 29–30
myocardial infarction, 40

N

negative sources, 60
negativity, 4, 55, 57

O

offense, 61, 65

P

pain, 2, 49, 65
passionate, 5, 42
peace, 26, 33, 52, 56, 69
post office, 7
power, 7, 28
prayer life, 26–27
prayers, 3, 12, 26, 28, 35, 41, 48, 52, 61, 73–74
praying, 1, 26
price, 43, 58
probation, 2

process, 11, 49
prophesy, 9, 12
prophet, 34, 59, 63, 74
prophetic word, 3, 56
provisions, 18, 56
python attack, 26

R

responsibilities, 53
revenge, 2, 65

S

scepter, 33
season, 42
secrets, 28, 32
self-esteem, 38
sexual sins, 32
sluggishness, 40
social life, 48
song, 64

T

television, 6, 32

temptation, 27
testimonials, 26
tongues, 26, 64

U

usher, 10, 29

V

Vegetables, 42
vindication, 70
vision, 17, 20, 62
vision building, 21
voice, 32
vow, 6, 9

W

warfare, 4
water, 39, 43
weight, 41
worship, 12, 29–30
worshipping, 35–36

Y

YouTube Videos, 25

www.ingramcontent.com/pod-product-compliance
Lightning Source LLC
Chambersburg PA
CBHW052117110526
44592CB00013B/1640